THE DEBEN RIVER

An Enchanted Waterway

BY ROBERT SIMPER

With additional material from Graham Henderson

Published in 1992 by Creekside Publishing, Suffolk
ISBN 0 9519927 0 8

By the same author:

Over Snape Bridge (1967)
Woodbridge & Beyond (1972)
East Coast Sail (1972)
Scottish Sail (1974)
North East Sail (1976)
British Sail (1977)
Victorian & Edwardian Yachting from Old Photographs (1978)
Gaff Sail (1979)
Traditions of East Anglia (1980)
Suffolk Show (1981)
Britain's Maritime Heritage (1982)
Sail on the Orwell (with Roger Finch) (1982)
Beach Boats of Britain (1984)
Sail. The Surviving Tradition (1984)
East Anglian Coast and Waterways (1985)
The Suffolk Sandlings (1986)

CONTENTS

Cover: *L'Atalanta* at her moorings in the Rocks Reach
during the 1987 hurricane.
Photograph by Jonathan Simper.

ACKNOWLEDGEMENTS

The River Deben means different things to different people. Some of the material gathered for this book came from people who are no longer with us, but their memories stretched back into the last century. Of these I have to mention the Woodbridge photographer W H Needs, and Arthur Hunt, yacht skipper and fisherman at Ramsholt who died in 1957. As a boy I used to go with Arthur helping him on the river and he talked freely about the days before World War I when every tide saw a barge going up river to Woodbridge. Conversations I had with Hervey Benham, amongst others, also helped to build up a picture of the Deben as a commercial highway.

Much of the information on Woodbridge came from Frank and Christine Knights. Other people who were helpful include Clifford and Rosemary Hoppitt, Caroline Cowper, Joan Whisstock, John Krejsa, Nicholas Minifie, Arthur E. Smith and R. F. Marsh. George Turner and Mick Nunn helped with Waldringfield. Thanks to John Newman, who has walked most of the villages looking for ancient settlements, to Bob Markham for background on the 1939 Sutton Hoo discovery, and to Gordon Kinsey. Peter Dolman helped with the Deben mills. Geoff Cordy did the photographic work. I am grateful to my daughter Caroline Southernwood for illustrations and to my wife Pearl for helping with the editing.

The idea of a book on the Deben came from Graham Henderson of Felixstowe Ferry, who also made material he had collected available.

R. S.
Ramsholt, 1992.

Sources of photograph illustrations

Clifford Hoppitt 3, 46, 53, 56, 61, 62, 72. East Anglian Daily Times 4, 49, 91, 109. Frank Hussey 11, 16, 17, 60. Nicholas Minifie 12, 21, 58, 104. R. F. Marsh 14. Suffolk Photo Survey 15, 23, 29, 30, 38, 50, 55, 64, 76, 77, 78, 96, 121. Aubrey Frost 19. Tate Gallery 22. Michael Spear 24, 25, 27, 28. Christine Knights 26, 93, 94, 95a, 97, 98, 123, 124, 125. Frederick Shimmon 31. Joan Whisstock 32, 51, 52, 65, 83, 85, 86. Peter Dolman 33, 35. Christine Bayly 39. Graham Henderson 42, 69, 71, 118, 120, 140, 141. Clive Southernwood 44. George Collins 68, 130. Pearl Simper 89. Rev. Leeder 107. Caroline Cowper 108, 110. R. S. Baker 117. George Turner 114. Trevor Woodall 126, 127. Woodbridge Cruising Club 135. John Smith 37a, 119a. Sixty-one photographs were taken by the author and the rest are from his collection.

Chapter One

ROYAL RIVER

ON A very low tide in the sea, off the Dip at Old Felixstowe, a few rocks can be seen which are marked on the old maps as Walton Castle. This is one of the few reminders that coastal Suffolk was once part of the Roman Empire and that the area had small Romano-British farms. The Romans had considerable trouble with Saxon pirates from northern Germany who came over and raided the coastal settlements of south east England. To combat this they built a chain of forts at strategic places which they backed up with a fleet of galleys which went out when pirates were known to be on the coast.

One of these forts, Portus Adurni, was built at the mouth of the Deben River to guard the Sandlings coast. That seems to have been rather an odd choice because Harwich Harbour has a much better deep water entrance and all major shipping activities in modern times have been centred here. Obviously Harwich Harbour has been greatly improved by dredging, but the Deben must have had some great advantage which has been lost, because all the early people were attracted to it. The answer was probably Goseford, which was then a sheltered creek behind Felixstowe. In bad weather the small oar and sail craft of the past would have found little shelter in the open Stour or Orwell, and in their search for a safe anchorage near the open sea Goseford would have been the best bet.

After the Roman army had left and returned to the European mainland the Angles and Saxons came across the North Sea and settled along all the rivers of Suffolk and Norfolk. These new Anglo-Saxon people soon began to war amongst themselves for control over the land they had occupied. Again control of the Deben seems to have been critical and holding it allowed one group of war lords, the Wuffings, to push out and create the new Kingdom of East Anglia. Although the Anglo-Saxons continued to use the abandoned Roman settlement on the Felixstowe Cliffs near the fort, this was too open to attack from the sea so the Wuffings made their headquarters inland at Rendlesham.

Besides this there was a Roman ford at Rendlesham, and to hold this gave them control over movements in the Sandlings. The name Ufford, meaning Wuffing's ford, suggests that by the end of the fifth century they had dominated first the upper River Deben crossing and finally the whole of East Anglia between the River Stour and the Fens. The early pagan Wuffings had their royal hall or palace at Rendlesham. This wooden hall probably stood on the present site of Naunton Hall and there was a huge 40 acre settlement site, the largest in the Deben valley, just to the north of the church.

Each of the early English kingdoms had its own market centre from which the king drew revenue. Ipswich, because of the wealth of the settlements in the Gipping valley and easy sea links to Rheinland market centres, soon became the centre of East Anglia. However the kings did not stay in one place, but constantly moved around. One of the places they are reputed to have held their courts was Debenham. In the days before maps and roads the head of a river made a recognized meeting place. From its source just above Debenham the fresh water Deben runs about ten miles down to Ufford and then another ten miles of tidal estuary down to the sea. According to the early Victorian *White's Dictionaries* there was once navigation on the Deben right up to Debenham and an anchor was even found in the river bed in the Gull just above the town.

It is quite possible that early medieval people did use the Deben to move bulk goods. Once the river was dammed to create mill ponds this would have been impracticable. In modern times Wickham Market mill and the weirs at Brandeston created water deep enough for anglers to stock with coarse fish, but Melton Mill weir ends most boating activity. On the estuary the early settlements were on the high ground overlooking the river near the 'gates' or creek landings. Later on villages grew up away from the river because the marshes caused marsh fever; the sea coast was avoided because of pirates.

Deben valley place names come from the early Anglo-Saxon settlers. Waldringfield was 'Field of the sons of Waldhere', Bawdsey was 'Baldhere's Island' and so on. It has been suggested that the old name for the river was Colne or Cole, but by the Elizabethan period the name Deben was in use and contemporary writers stated it took the name from the fresh water river coming down from Debenham. Until Victorian times it was generally called Deben River, or simply the Channel, while coasting seamen called it the Woodbridge River leading up from Woodbridge Haven at Felixstowe Ferry.

The tidal River Deben the early medieval

people knew was very different to the one we sail on. First the entrance appears to have been slightly to the south by the ruins of the Roman fort which was rebuilt in the medieval period as Walton Castle. However the sea eroded both Walton Castle and the headland to the south on which had been the Roman and Anglo-Saxon settlements, while to the north probably several hundred yards of Bawdsey Cliffs have gone into the sea.

The mouth of the river has moved constantly, but the depth of water in the channel over the Bar across the mouth seems to have stayed around 4ft at low water. On high water spring tides near the present Horse Buoy the river would have been three miles wide between Alderton and Trimley. This was completely changed by walling off the saltings to make summer grazing marshes. The labour needed to hand dig the river walls must have been great, but it was worth it because during the dry summers the grazing on the high ground died off while the grass kept growing on the new marshes because of their high water table.

Walling up the saltings for cattle grazing took place very slowly and had started before 1200 in the lower reaches; the last walls seem to have been completed above Woodbridge in the early 1600s. The Falkenham, Alderton and the Ramsholt Dock Marshes had several sets of walls showing that the river was pushed back in separate ventures. Walling took place so slowly that the river did not alter much in a man's lifetime, but it did dramatically alter the Deben, making it a much narrower river.

Goseford remained an important anchorage in medieval times and ships owned in Bawdsey and Walton were referred to as belonging to the Port of Goseford. Walton Hall was a royal manor, and this was used as an assembly point in 1338 by King Edward III for his army before sailing to attack Flanders. Some of this fleet gathered in Goseford Haven, but the flag ship was round in the Orwell.

Silting has gradually closed the Deben creeks to shipping, but Goseford Haven must have silted up rapidly once the saltings on either side had been walled off because there was then little current to sweep the silt away. Goseford was finally closed to save the cost of maintaining the long length of river wall on either side. Once it was walled off the name changed to King's Fleet (fleet means shallow in Suffolk), and it remains a great favourite with anglers. On the opposite shore of the Deben, the Fleet which leads up to Alderton brick kiln was open until the 1860s when horses were towing coal barges up there. This creek had once made Bawdsey an island by

joining up with Hollesley Haven, but it does not appear to have ever been deep enough for ships to get through. Falkenham and Kirton Creeks remain, but when cut off from their former full length they silted badly and only Martlesham remains a creek which is navigable.

The last time the Deben took on its medieval size was after the 1953 East Coast Floods when an abnormally high tide burst over the low grass river walls and flooded all the marshes. The Government had to make a massive investment to rebuild the walls and to justify it encouraged farmers to plough up the old grazing and turn the marshes over to wheat production. However, the Hemley Hall marshes opposite the Rocks had already been abandoned to the tide after a very bitter legal battle. These marshes were flooded by a high tide in about 1940 and the River Board refused to accept responsibility for repairing the walls. The farmer at Hemley Hall won the first two court hearings against the River Board, but the House of Lords reversed these findings. The Hemley Point wall remained unrepaired and the farmer had to sell up to pay the court costs. After this several of the small areas of marshes beside upper reaches in Martlesham and Sutton also returned to tidal water again.

People have lived in organized communities along the Deben for at least three thousand years and their farming practices and social aspirations have constantly altered the valley. It is still bordered by farmland, but the layout is completely man made. However it comes as a surprise to read an account in a Victorian magazine of 1885 about the beauty of the heathland sweeping down to the edge of the Deben. A tiny patch of the great heathland belt which once stretched right through to Snape is on top of the Ramsholt Dock cliff, while the last heath to go on the Sutton shore was engulfed by Little Haddon Hall when it was built in 1914; the remainder near Methersgate Hall was ploughed up in about 1955. Because much of the high land around the tidal Deben was once open heath there were few trees along the river a century ago. Many of the woods and belts that can now be seen were originally planted between the 1870s and 1914 as pheasant cover.

In the 1870s there were no trees at Kingston, the low headland leading down to Kyson Point at the mouth of Martlesham Creek. Kingston, which means king's farm, is a place of great mystery. At least a little is known about Sutton Hoo and Rendlesham, but nothing has been found of the royal manor at Kingston. The valley of the River Finn above Martlesham was thickly populated by the Anglo-Saxons and the good natural landing at Kyson Point would have been an obvious place for them to land their goods.

In the early history of the Deben the centres of power and trade moved around, but they finally settled at Woodbridge, at the highest point a merchant vessel could easily reach. The actual town of Woodbridge began up on the Market Hill. This may have been a late Anglo-Saxon burh, a place fortified against attack from the Vikings. Once the medieval weekly market was started Woodbridge grew to be the commercial centre of the district, and the centre of local justice was moved here from Melton in the Elizabethan period.

Although there were few trees in the Sandlings, inland High Suffolk was full of oaks which were brought to Woodbridge for export or shipbuilding in the town. By the Elizabethan period the size of ship was increasing and they were being sold to London merchants. In 1566 the 120 ton *Bark Smith* was launched into the Deben, and by 1604 the largest to have been built at Woodbridge was the 290 ton *Ann Francis*. There was not a ship of this size built again until 1616 when the 292 ton *Palmer* and 326 ton *Centurion* were launched. A decade later the golden age of Woodbridge shipping started and between 1625 and 1638 eleven large ships were built including *Levent Merchant* and *Muscovy Merchant*, both of 400 tons, and the *Goodman* of 1634, which was 700 tons. The Woodbridge builders were awarded contracts to build ships for the Royal Navy, the largest of which was the 663 ton *Kingfisher* in 1675. After this ships built at Woodbridge decreased in size.

Although most of the Deben's past has been very peaceful, whenever there was war or instability in Europe the Suffolk coast was in the front line. The ambitions of Napoleon's France led to Woodbridge becoming a garrison town between 1794 and 1814, while down at the Deben mouth three Martello Towers were built about 1810 to guard the entrance. Another century of peace ended when Germany tried to use force in two World Wars to dominate Europe. A few pillboxes are the only reminder that during World War II the whole coast was heavily fortified against invasion and attack from the air.

Bawdsey Manor was in the forefront of the new aerial warfare because it was bought by the Government in 1935 and used to develop radar. For over fifty years the sound of war planes was familiar in the sky above the Deben. They were in deadly earnest, with RAF fighters from Martlesham airfield defending against the raiding German planes. Then came the US Air Force flying from their hastily built airfields to bomb Germany into submission. In the following forty-five years after this there were US war planes and helicopters from the Bentwaters and Woodbridge bases which never fired a shot in anger, but were still a vital part of the Cold War which led to the collapse of communist USSR.

Even the battle for the air waves just touched the Deben when in 1964 Radio Caroline, the first pirate radio station, was anchored off East Lane just outside the limits of Britain's territorial waters. Deben boat owners sailed out and had pop music requests played, and when this station linked up with another Radio Caroline in the Irish Sea it was briefly the world's largest commercial radio station.

For centuries trade, shipbuilding, defence and a little fishing were the main occupations of the river but there were a few yachts in the background. It seems that there were boats for pleasure sailing in the area by the 1740s, while the first recorded Deben race, between the *Temple* and the *Flora*, took place in 1784 from Woodbridge Common Quay (Ferry Dock) to Bawdsey and back. The Woodbridge Regatta was started in 1838 with sailing and rowing races. Most of the little group of yachts moored off the Ferry Dock belonged to Woodbridge's tradesmen and minor gentry, who walked down to the river from their homes in the town.

It was the internal combustion engine that changed the Deben, and this happened in three separate ways. In the 1920s small mass-produced cars made it possible for people living in local towns to drive down to boats at Waldringfield, Felixstowe Ferry and even down the pot-holed lane to Ramsholt Dock. Because of the strong tides over the Bar at the river entrance many boat owners avoided the Deben, but in the 1960s reliable engines were fitted in almost all yachts and these made the Deben easily accessible.

In 1962 the yawl *Giselle of Iken* was the first yacht with a fibreglass hull to be kept on the Deben. The use of fibreglass allowed yachts to be mass produced and in the next couple of decades the Deben was transformed from a remote backwater to a major recreational area. The Deben was very attractive to owners because the moorings here were cheap, so boat numbers rose at a relentless pace. Between 1976 and 1990 the numbers of boats kept on moorings, mud berths and marinas increased at the rate of 44 boats a year to about 1571.

When the first yachts appeared each anchorage had been the closely guarded territory of watermen who controlled the moorings, but as boat numbers shot up, this system began to break down. The yacht clubs, commercial boatyards and local government all claimed that they should be responsible for managing the river. However the Deben had always been a free river and even the Lords of the Manor had no authority over the tideway. The boat owners wanted it to remain an open river, but opinion was bitterly divided over how this was to be achieved. There were protectionists who fought to retain the old tradition of total freedom, and there were those who wanted mooring committees to organize the fairways. Usually the situation reached a point where moorings started to appear in the main channel, and then a mooring committee was set up to lease the river bed from the Crown Commissioners. At least the semi-democratic mooring committees have kept the channel clear and some reaches free of moorings.

The Suffolk Coastal District Council had a chance to extend some control over the tidal Deben when they imposed a speed limit. The speed limit came as a result of public protest, but the first time the Deben boat owners flexed their muscles was in 1963 when a Frenchman, Monsieur Gouzer, applied for permission from the Ministry of Agriculture and Fisheries to start to cultivate oysters between Green Point and Early Creek.

When M. Gouzer came up with his plan there was massive opposition from just about every boat owner. The Deben Protection Group was formed to fight 'the Frenchman'. Although many protesters were as much anti-French as anti-oysters, any attempt at stopping boats anchoring or trawling in any part of the river was seen as the loss of an ancient liberty. The matter resolved itself when a hard winter wiped out M. Gouzer's trial oysters and he wisely retired back to his native land without further ado. When in 1974 Robert Brinkley, a Felixstowe Ferry fisherman, applied for permission to lay oysters the Deben Protection Group came back into life to fight the application. However because it was a local man this time many river users were reluctant to protest; an attempt was made in the Falkenham Reach to cultivate oysters, but it faded out.

In the Deben's new role as a leisure area all the attention was focused on maintaining the rights of pleasure boat owners. A new approach came in 1990 when Annie Healey set in motion the formation of the River Deben Association with the aim of involving all the people who derived a living from the river and those who wanted to protect the Deben in working out a common policy for the future. The RDA's first tangible success was when its members went out along the tide line and picked up several tons of rubbish, the unwanted fruits of many boat owners' leisure time afloat.

The importance of the Deben as a wild life habitat seems to have been late to be recognized. Nearly a third of all the saltings in Suffolk are on the Deben, with Hemley Point just below Waldringfield being the largest single area of saltings in the county. The need to maintain this habitat led in 1991 to most of the saltings between Bromeswell Common and Felixstowe Ferry being declared a Site of Special Scientific Interest. Any move to protect this small but truly lovely estuary seems worth while. However the centuries have been kind to the Deben and much of it has a timeless quality. Twice a day the tide floods and ebbs and takes little notice of the affairs of people.

Chapter Two

SUTTON HOO

IN THE summer of 1939, just a few weeks before the outbreak of World War II, one of the most important discoveries in British archaeological history was made beside the Deben. One of the mounds at Sutton Hoo was opened revealing the pagan burial of Raedwald, King of East Anglia, who died about 625. This great warrior king had been the over king of all the Anglo-Saxon kingdoms at a time when the new English nation was just taking shape.

The Sutton Hoo House, which stands on the hilltop overlooking Woodbridge, was built in 1910 and purchased in 1926 by the Prettys, members of an Ipswich family. Just to the south of the house on the highest hilltop over looking the Deben were a series of ancient mounds. In 1862 the local landowner, Mr Barrett, had dug into the mounds. No record has survived of Barrett's finds except a brief mention in the local paper of a 'bushel of shipscews'. By the time the Prettys bought Sutton Hoo Barrett had been forgotten, although there was a legend in Woodbridge that the mounds contained a ship-burial.

Mrs Edith Pretty was very curious about the origins of the mounds on her Sutton Hoo estate. It was her firm belief that one moonlight night she had seen the ghost of a great warrior standing on Mound One. Convinced that the group of mounds contained something of great importance, she asked Ipswich Museum to dig them. This museum suggested she employed Basil Brown, a local man with skill at interpreting the soil, to excavate them. When in 1939 Brown and Mrs Pretty's gardener and gamekeeper dug into Mound One they were amazed to find traces of a huge open longship buried there. This ship turned out to be 89ft long, in fact far larger than any other ship found in a Germanic pagan ship-burial. To aid the digging Guy Maynard, curator of Ipswich Museum, began research into other ship-burials and a rumour went around the academic world that something very important was about to be discovered on a lonely patch of Suffolk heathland.

Charles Phillips of Cambridge University came down to Sutton Hoo and received authority to be in charge of the excavation of Mound One. Basil Brown remained working on the Sutton Hoo site, but it was Phillips and his team who unearthed the burial chamber in the centre of the ship. In this wooden chamber they found all the everyday household goods an Anglo-Saxon king would need for his journey into the 'after world'

and treasure, which proclaimed his very high status. From the dating of the gold buckle, silver plate and coins it would seem that the burial had taken place in about 625, meaning that it must have been Raedwald, the most powerful of the Kings of East Anglia, who had been buried here.

To prevent treasure seekers raiding the site Phillips demanded that the finds at Sutton Hoo be kept secret. However Mr Fairweather, proprietor and editor of the 'Woodbridge Reporter', heard about the finds and asked to be able to print an account, but Phillips refused. Soon the 'East Anglian Daily Times' asked if they could print the story, but although the public were freely visiting the site Phillips still kept the media at bay. By this time the London papers had picked up the story and Ipswich Museum, who felt the site was their responsibility, confirmed to the London press that a major treasure had been found. Without further delay the 'East Anglian Daily Times' ran the story and a furious Phillips threatened to go into Ipswich and horse-whip the editor. The poor old 'Woodbridge Reporter' was rewarded for its silence by coming out with the story last.

There were other bitter local confrontations. The president of the Ipswich Museum, James Reid Moir, considered Sutton Hoo to be their discovery and wanted the treasure displayed in Ipswich. Phillips used Mrs Pretty's Spiritualist mentor to influence her into making the British Museum the final home of the Sutton Hoo treasure. The actual finder of the Sutton Hoo ship-burial, Basil Brown, spent the rest of his life locating new archaeological sites in Suffolk, but he always felt that influential academics had come in and taken his glory. However towards the end of his life it began to be fully recognized that it was Basil Brown's skill which had traced out the shape of the Mound One ship in the acidic Suffolk sand.

After World War II, Dr Rupert Bruce-Mitford made a long academic study of the Sutton Hoo finds and between 1965 and 1970 some exploration took place on the site, mainly to try to get further details about Mound One. This work did not throw much light on the origins of this royal burial field. It was nearly fifty years after the famous 1939 discoveries before there was a major attempt to resolve the origins of Sutton Hoo. From 1983 to 1991 a series of digs carefully investigated parts of the site and the results were interpreted by the project leader, Professor Martin Carver.

The acidic sand of Sutton Walks did not give

up its ancient secrets willingly. Worse still the Research Project found that all the large mounds had been robbed. Most disappointing was Mound Two, which was found to have been robbed even before Basil Brown had dug there. However painstaking research did reveal that there had been another ship-burial in Mound Two, probably destroyed by Barrett, which must have been just as rich as the Mound One discovery in 1939. In the case of Mound Two the long ship had been placed on the top of the burial chamber. The finds around Mound Six were even more extraordinary because they contained the graves of human sacrifices.

Another interesting discovery was the reason why Mound One had survived when most of the main mounds had been robbed. At some time, probably during the food shortages in the Napoleonic Wars, the site had been ploughed. During this time dust storms could have blown one end of Mound One away. When Mr Barrett or some other grave robber dug on the site they missed the burial chamber because the centre was no longer in the original place. Ploughing also saved Mound Seventeen. This was nothing more than a slight bump and was dug literally in the last days of the eight year campaign. Although it was kept secret it was to everyone's great excitement that at last a mound had been found that had not been robbed. Here lay a young warrior complete with sword, spear, shield and decorated bridle. A few feet away buried in another grave was his horse.

Sutton Hoo was the burial show place of a powerful royal family who had contacts throughout the British Isles and Europe. They felt threatened by the Christianity pushing its way up from the Latin south and they wanted to retain their Germanic pagan religion. The young prince in Mound Seventeen and King Raedwald had, following the pagan custom, been buried on a headland, in this case the highest land beside the Deben, where their burial mounds were outlined against the sky and would have impressed the early Anglo-Saxons that this mighty family had the right to rule over the area.

1. In 1939 an 89ft long ship was found in Mound One at Sutton Hoo. This ship was built of oak which had been split, not sawn, into planks. Jake Hussey's drawing shows the burial chamber of Raedwald, King of East Anglia, amidships.

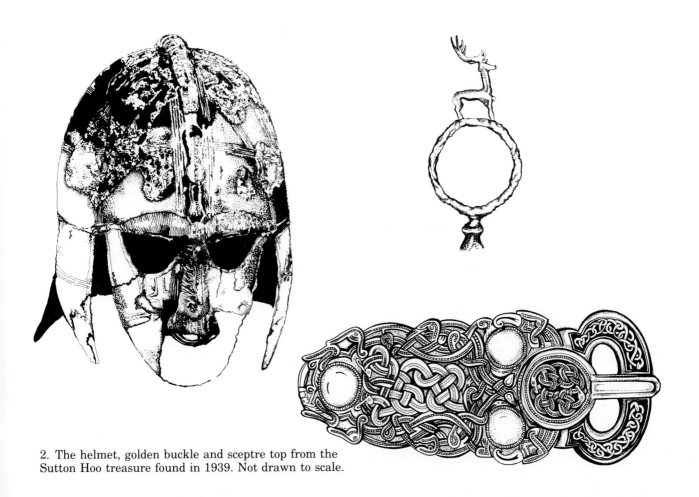

2. The helmet, golden buckle and sceptre top from the
Sutton Hoo treasure found in 1939. Not drawn to scale.

3. Cliff Hoppitt's aerial
photograph of the royal
burial field at Sutton
Hoo in April 1987 shows
the excavations on
Mound Two. The light
patch in Bill Waring's
field in the foreground
had been excavated and
there appeared to be
human sacrifices buried
around a sacred tree.

7

4. The acid soil at Sutton Hoo had only left a dark stain in the soil which marked where both the ships and bodies were. Seen here in 1984 is a Sutton Hoo 'sandman', just the carefully excavated trace of a body.

5. In the centre is the Duke of Edinburgh, President of the Sutton Hoo Society, visiting the excavation in 1987. On the left is Project Director Professor Martin Carver and on the right, Site Supervisor Andy Copp.

6. In the autumn of 1991, in the very last days of the eight year long excavations, Mound Seventeen, which was little more than a slight rise in the ground, was found to contain unrobbed graves of a young prince and his horse.

7. In 1986 Angela Evans of the British Museum explains the excavation of Mound Two, seen in the background. This mound had contained an important ship-burial but at some point had been robbed.

8. Professor Martin Carver with Mound Two being reconstructed in 1992. Professor Carver believes that the Sutton Hoo mounds had been levelled at some stage so after the excavations he had all the soil from this mound and its quarry ditch put back as the Anglo-Saxons would have completed the burial mound.

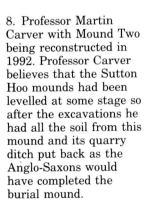

9

Chapter Three

TRADE ON THE DEBEN

WOODBRIDGE was the market centre of the Sandlings area and the port of registration for the commercial and fishing vessels of the Deben, Ore and Alde rivers. In the early decades of the nineteenth century there were seventy vessels totalling 5000 tons registered at Woodbridge. About forty, mostly trading vessels, were owned in Woodbridge. The town was a thriving country port with about 20,000 tons a year 'going over' its quays. Coal came from the north of England, linseed cake for cattle feed from Liverpool, timber from the Baltic ports and wine, spirits, groceries and general goods from London. The main exports were corn, flour, hardwood trees and general agricultural goods. It was said that Woodbridge exported 'the best butter in England, and perhaps some of the worst cheese'.

The first Customs House was built on Woodbridge Quay in 1589 but the later Customs House in Quay Street was closed in 1882. Dues were collected here for the wines and spirits which were stored in bonded warehouses. The one in Tide Mill Way survives as the scout headquarters. Quay Street leading down to the Ferry Dock was the heart of the little sailing ship port of Woodbridge. Here in the 'Anchor' the master mariners and shareholders met to talk over shipping affairs while round the corner the sailors drank at the 'Boat Inn'. Just up in Church Street Barclays Bank, which has been a bank since 1797, was the home of the banker Alexander, who lent the capital for Taylor to build new trading schooners at the Lime Kiln yard and held mortgages on the shares of many local vessels.

The ownership of British vessels is divided into 64 shares and to spread the risk people had shares in several vessels. Although several Woodbridge schooners were registered as being owned by Trott & Co, in fact George and William Trott of Castle Street only held some shares in them and acted as managers. Sailors used to talk of a ship 'belonging to Woodbridge' this would mean she was probably built here, and even the ropes and sail cloth were made in the town. It was a very close knit community where the banker, shareholders, masters and crews knew each other personally, even if they did not mix socially. Since these small sailing vessels were at the mercy of the wind and weather there was constant loss of life, which caused hardship. The Woodbridge Shipwreck Society, which lasted nearly seventy years and received donations from wealthy residents, was run by a committee of seafaring men.

The nineteenth century brigs and schooners drew around 10ft of water and when deeply loaded had to wait until the 'spring' tides (which came every fortnight) to get up to Woodbridge. The foreign timber ships bound for Lime Kiln Quay had thirty tons taken out into lighters at Kyson Point. Even then these deep draught schooners had a problem getting into the Ferry Dock, and there are accounts of sixteen men working on a schooner's windlass to drag her through the mud up to the quay. Leaving also had its problems because the schooners could not sail without taking on about 40 ton of ballast.

After the railway reached Woodbridge in 1859 most of the business people in the district lost interest in shipping. The shipyard closed and as local schooners were lost or sold they were not replaced, but the arrival of sailing barges gave trade on the river a new lease of life. The barges were flat bottomed and shallow draft, which made them quicker getting up the river; they did not need ballast; and they had smaller crews so they were cheaper to operate. Sadly very few barges were owned in the Deben.

Barges changed the pattern of trade on the river. The schooner trade was almost all to the wharves at Woodbridge, but the barges with their flat bottoms took on cargoes at a whole range of new farm wharves or 'docks' along the river. For the haulage of bulk cargoes, such as grain and coal, barges could always undercut the expensive railways. Barges were supplying local needs but not expanding the port. There was an attempt to try to save the port by digging Loder's Cut in 1879. This was done to save time beating up through the narrow Troublesome Reach against the southwesterlies coming down Martlesham Creek.

Shipping lost time getting over the Deben bar and even with Loder's Cut there were often delays getting up the shallow upper reaches. A programme of dredging was needed to save the port of Woodbridge, but the trade into the river did not generate enough revenue. In the 1920s lorries took over the the local haulage and it was cheaper to ship goods into Ipswich and bring it over land. The trade into the Deben died quite quickly. Until about 1930 barges and small steamers were coming regularly; then quite suddenly the wharves were all empty and the river left to a tiny handful of yachtsmen, fishermen and wildfowlers.

9. This view of the Woodbridge riverside about 1812 appears to be the head of the Ferry Dock, with a trading sloop laid up.

Between 1720 and 1820 the great unseen trade of the Deben was smuggling. The smugglers were hard men who used force when necessary. The Shottisham smuggler William Richardson was wanted for murder and had to flee the country to join the outlaws' colony at Flushing. Usually the smuggling gangs did not have to use force because they had the full cooperation of most of the local people at every level of society. Also the Customs men were badly undermanned when dealing with the smuggling gangs. In 1777 a Customs Collector dryly reported 'We generally see Bawdsey men among the smugglers, every week there is a landing close to where the Bawdsey Prevention boat is stationed' (possibly hinting that the Customs men at Woodbridge Haven were being given a tip to turn a blind eye to activities of the Free Traders). Sometimes the Customs were lucky, such as when a smuggler's boat ran aground on the Deben Bar in 1738 and they were able to seize all the tea and brandy aboard. However, after a court hearing a sympathetic judge gave the smugglers their goods back!

The Customs cutters chased any craft thought to be smuggling. Once they pursued a vessel up the Deben, only to lose it when the smugglers threw their cannons overboard in Troublesome Reach so that their lighter vessel was able to go on up river when the customs cutter grounded. Another time a Customs cutter chased a smuggling craft to Ramsholt. Cart tracks were then followed across a field to where barrels of spirits were hidden underground, but at this point nearly a hundred armed smugglers appeared and 'beat the Customs Officers in a very barbarous manner'.

Martlesham Creek, which must have silted up, seems to have been a favourite landing place. Phillip Meadows, rector of Great Bealings, used to leave his stables open with his chaise harness ready for use and the smugglers used it to collect goods landed at Martlesham Creek. The same story is told of the rector of Martlesham who lived just beside the creek. When the Martlesham rector's horse and carriage was used by the smugglers he hid in the bushes to make sure they left the customary keg as payment.

At Alderton the church was linked by a tunnel to the near-by farmhouse; no doubt the rector here was also never short of brandy. It was remembered by the Cross family who farmed at Hemley Hall for over a century after 1770 that they used to go into their stables in the morning and find their horses sweating after being used by the smugglers during the night. Another farming family handed down the story that once when walking on the Kirton Marshes with his family a farmer suddenly bent down and picked up a little keg from under a bridge. This was the farmer's payoff for allowing his horses to be used by the smugglers. For those who did not cooperate there was always the threat of the 'bobbing lights'. This was a story put about by the smugglers that there were ghosts out on the marshes. In fact if you looked closely at the 'bobbing lights' you were more likely to get a bang on the head by the bad boys of Bawdsey than by anything supernatural.

10. The Newsons' pleasure boat taking a party on a trip from Felixstowe Ferry up to Woodbridge in about 1905.

When smuggling faded out fishermen of Woodbridge Haven took to pilotage and salvaging as a lucrative sideline. In the days of small sailing ships they were at the mercy of weather and with poor charts were always needing assistance. In 1816 Henry Newson, master of the Felixstowe Ferry salvage smack *John & Hannah*, got into trouble for piloting a vessel into Harwich after showing the licences of his father-in-law James Passiful. The Newsons and Passifuls seem to have dominated affairs at the Deben mouth for about a century.

By the 1870s Ablet Passiful was repeatedly earning large salvage claims with his smacks *Violet* and *Wonder* and he also organized a beach company at Felixstowe Ferry. The beach companies were fishermen's cooperatives which saved lives and salvaged vessels in trouble. The Passiful salvage yawl, known as 'the galley', was officially called the *Pride of the Deben* and was kept hauled out in front of the Martello Tower. 'Settler' Newson remembered her being there in the early 1900s; his father had been in charge of her. They used Quilter's horses to launch the yawl, and his father recalled coming back from a wreck on the Shipwash Sands with the yawl loaded with cutlery, whisky and a piano and with most of the crew happy but lying dead drunk in the bottom of the boat.

The last of the old style salvages must have been in 1915, when against the orders of the Royal Navy the Ferry men went out and took the gear out of a steamer ashore on the Shipwash. The lifeboats of the RNLI put most salvage companies out of business, but the Felixstowe Ferry fishermen continued the traditions of the salvagers in a small way by giving assistance to yachtsmen ashore on the Deben Bar. The old salvage yawls were often converted to pleasure boats as pleasure trips took the place of salvaging.

11. Pilot Billy Newson waiting to pilot Frank Hussey's yacht over the Deben Bar in 1930. Billy Newson was a Deben pilot until 1961 and his cousin Ted 'Settler' Newson went on for another year to be the last official pilot. In 1879 the seven pilots at the Ferry were bringing in barges at the rate of 15–20 a month. Billy's father Charlie remembered seeing fourteen barges waiting at sea to come over the Deben Bar on the same tide; Settler's father had brought in square-rigged ships with timber from Russia and grain from Canada. The last steamer 'Settler' brought in drew 12ft of water in a channel which was only a few inches deeper, and he said he would not do it again.

When bringing sailing barges in against a head wind the pilot brought them up to the bar channel and then threw the head up into the wind and let the roaring tide sweep them into the river. When the weather was bad and the pilots could not row out, they anchored on the inside of the channel and signalled with flags to show the skipper which way to sail.

12. The Woodbridge smack *Jem Mace* belonged to the Woodbridge pilot Peter Broom. Before 1882 the Woodbridge smacks carried the registration letters WE. The Woodbridge pilots went fishing or helped discharge barges, but when a vessel was known to be in the river they rowed down river to meet them.

13. The pilot skiff *Teddy* is the oldest Woodbridge-built boat in existence. She was built about 1877 by a builder in Brook Street and used by pilot Ted Marsh and his father before him to row down river.

14

14. Ted Marsh (1877–1959) in his official uniform as Trinity House pilot, although he did not wear this to bring up barges. Born in the 'Boat Inn', he went to sea at the age of twelve in barges and billyboys out of Woodbridge. Later Captain Passiful of Woodbridge asked him and another local man to go deep sea and he went round Cape Horn four times in the 4-masted barque *Achnashie*. He returned to Woodbridge to become a pilot with Nelson Oxborrow. As Out Port pilots they were licensed to take a vessel from a mile seaward of the Bar to Wilford Bridge, but they usually left the entrance to the Ferry men and met the barges coming up river. Ted brought the last commercial craft up to Woodbridge. This was the steamer *Maloo* in 1940, which had to wait at Waldringfield because of the ice before going to Sun Wharf. In 1947 Ted retired as pilot and Frank Knights took on the position and brought up yachts when requested.

15. A coprolite washing plant on the site of the present Waldringfield Sailing Club. Over a thousand tons of coprolite was dug from the fields around the 'Maybush' and shipped from the beach by barge to the Ipswich crushing mills. Coprolite, a mixture of fossilized animal bones and droppings, was crushed to make superphosphate of lime fertilizer. Since coprolite was found near the surface in the Suffolk Sandlings, digging started along the Deben in 1845 and soon developed into a local boom industry. At its height in the 1870s about 10,000 tons a year was being shipped from the Deben and Orwell quays to Ipswich, but once imported fertilizer appeared digging declined and the last pit is said to have closed in 1892. Coprolite led to the fertilizer manufacturing industry beginning in Ipswich. In the building boom of the 1980s many of the old coprolite pits were filled in with waste and few now remain.

16. Trading schooners at Woodbridge in about 1858. Since then most of the quays here have silted up many feet.

17. The tops'l schooner *Bernard Barton* laid up at Lime Kiln Quay in the 1880s. A typical Woodbridge schooner, she was launched at this yard in 1840 and named after the town's Quaker bank clerk who was enjoying fame as a poet. Under Captain William Passiful she traded to Liverpool but in 1880 was trading with cement from Waldringfield.

18. Brigantine at Woodbridge, about 1900. The First Shelter and beach replaced Jessup's warehouses.

19. Captain Douse of Woodbridge on the boomie (ketch barge) *Empress of India* at the Tide Mill Dock, about 1907. This 85ft barge was tiller steered and traded regularly as a collier to Woodbridge. Household coal came from the north of England and steam coal from south Wales.

The schooners and boomie barges were very difficult to turn to windward in the upper reaches, so often their crews rowed their boat with a line to the bowsprit end and towed the vessels down river. At the Deben Bar they put the barge alongside the Knolls and loaded shingle, which was often just shovelled down a chute. This shingle was sold in the north for building new docks. It was a poor freight, but 'just enough to fill the grub locker'.

20. This topsail schooner is making way up the Deben on a windless day by being kedged. Two anchors were used; one was rowed ahead and dropped and then the crew hauled the ship forward helped by the tide.

21. A view from Sutton Ferry across to Woodbridge, about 1895.

22. The Woodbridge artist Thomas Churchyard captured a swim-head spritsail barge across the Pan at the Lime Kiln yard about 1850. The Woodbridge mariners, who were used to little square-riggers making long voyages, called barges 'ditch crawlers' when they first appeared here in the 1840s, but soon these shallow draft craft rejuvenated trade on the river.

23. The ketch *Hope* entering the Bowships Reach, above the Rocks Reach; this was bound up river in the Victorian era before the estate owners started planting trees. The *Hope*, Captain Moss, was owned by Rowlands, the ironmonger in Woodbridge Thoroughfare, and she brought household goods and lamp oil, which was stored in a tank near the swimming pool, from the Thames. She finished trading about 1913 and her hull is under the mud ooze above Sun Wharf.

24. Five spritties (spritsail barges) in the Ferry Dock, another sprittie on the Bush End with the rowing ferry boat going in astern of her and two boomie barges over in the Mill Dock. On the left is the *Deben* owned by Fred Read of Woodbridge. This barge was the Woodbridge 'hoy' running a regular service to London until she was sold in 1911.

25. The Ferry Dock in the early 1920s: the three types of sailing craft then trading to Woodbridge. Nearest is the sprittie barge *Raybel* discharging barley in sacks which were taken by horse and cart up to the Crown Maltings. Behind her is a billyboy, a barge type which belonged to the Humber, though several were owned in Woodbridge, and behind her is the boomie barge *Ethel Edith*.

Apart from a hand crane for loading trees at the Ferry Dock all the cargoes on the Deben were handled by hand labour. The Woodbridge 'humpers', labourers hired by the day, and the vessel's own crews made up a gang of six men who usually took about a day and a half to discharge a 120 ton barge.

26. Four spritties at Wilford Bridge about 1901. Bargemen considered this was an easy place to sail or pole their way up to because the Deben pilots were very good at getting up river. The first Wilford Bridge was probably built on the ford in about 1575 and replaced by the present bridge in 1937.

27. A spritsail barge discharging road making material at Wilford Bridge in 1909.

28. Four spritsail barges at Melton Dock and another in the distance leaving Wilford Wharf in 1909.

29. A tiller steered barge discharging 'London mixture', horse muck from street horses, on Waldringfield beach about 1910. This was very unpopular in the village because of the smell of the cart loads going up the road. The barges returned with a 'stackie' freight, with heavy mangolds in the hold and then a stack of hay or straw on the deck reaching half way up the main mast.

30. Waldringfield beach with cement works kilns and barges in the background. Mason owned seven barges, of which only the *Orinoco* was still sailing in 1992.

31. The steamer *Esperanto* discharging in the Tide Mill Creek about 1925.

24

Opposite above: 32. Woodbridge Tide Mill working about 1930. Before the mill became a source of inspiration to artists it ground wheat into flour powered by tidal water trapped in a pond. When the tide fell the water was released to power the mill wheel. The post on the right was to help warp barges out of the creek. After the mill pond was closed the creek silted up.

The Tide Mill was probably built about 1793 and the Granary shortly afterwards. The Tide Mill's claim to fame is that by the time it finally stopped grinding in 1954 it was the last tide mill in operation in Britain. The mill was lucky to survive decades of neglect and was restored in 1975. The Granary was heightened and rebuilt as flats in 1991.

Opposite below: 33. Melton Mill in about 1896. The water mill at Melton is mentioned in the Domesday Book, when it was owned by the Abbot of Ely. The freshwater Deben at Ufford Bridge is diverted along a banked up channel to the mill. Eel traps were beside the wheel here, which was driven by an 8ft fall of water. The top of the tidal Deben flows up a second channel to the mill weir.

Below: 34. The Shottisham water mill about 1912. This mill stopped work in 1952 and was converted to a private house in 1985. The mill was powered by the Shottisham Mill Run, a stream leading down to Shottisham Creek. Another water mill on an eastern tributary of the Deben was the cloth making mill at Bromeswell Common, which appears to have had a small pond on the stream coming down from the Dirty Fen.

The River Finn, which flows down to Martlesham Creek, powered small medieval mills and the last one working on this river was the Playford Mill, which operated until about 1875. A tree then blocked the river and neither the tenant nor the estate owner would clear it so the mill was converted to cottages. On the Bucklesham Mill River going down to Kirton Creek the last water mill was at the present waterworks, but it seems that once there was also one just below Brightwell. The mill at Trimley was on the stream leading down to King's Fleet, but even the stream has dried up here.

On the freshwater Deben there were small medieval mills above Kettleburgh Mill, which have also gone. Kirby's map marks two mills at Letheringham and the surviving one was built in 1740 on the site of the smaller Domesday mill and operated until 1927. It had its wheel restored in 1990 and was opened to the public. The wheel at Glevering Mill was used to pump water up to the big house. The Campsey Ash Mill still has its machinery but is now a private house which has some timbers going back to the fifteenth century. All traces of Eyke mill have gone but it was near the ford. The Ufford Mill stopped working in 1916 and the last miller at Melton Mill left in 1896.

The last water mill to be commercially operated on the Deben was Rackham's Deben Mill at Wickham Market. It was in use up to 1972 and all the stones and machinery were still intact twenty years later. It took 2½ hours to grind a ton of wholemeal flour at the Deben Mill, and once there was enough flow in the river to power the mill for 24 hours a day except in a very dry summer. There was trouble at the Deben Mill with the poor fall of water. This was made worse in the late 1960s when the flow was considerably decreased in the summer by water being taken out for irrigation ponds. In 1991 during the longest drought in recorded history, when the freshwater Deben looked like drying out altogether, the NRA banned farmers from taking water out of the river.

Successive generations have found different uses for the Deben. There are seven sewage farms which allow their 'run off' to go out into the Deben, but both the freshwater and tidal rivers are, compared to the rest of Britain, still very good quality water. Fortunately the Deben has never had heavy industry or a large population to cause real damage to the environment and for most of its course the river runs through unspoilt farmland.

35. The gentleman punting on the Melton Mill pond in about 1905 is probably Charles Henry Fitzroy, who converted the mill to his private house. In 1992 this scene had changed little except that most of the buildings on the right had gone and the small barn was being converted to a 'Grandad annex'.

36. Reeds being 'combed' at Ramsholt in 1990 before being made into 'bolts' or bundles. Cutting reeds for thatching died out on the Deben but a Stowmarket thatcher revived it in the 1970s. Reed cutting takes place during the winter after a hard frost has killed the grass. The reed beds are cut at Ramsholt, Martlesham and on Nick Green's saltings below Bromeswell Common.

26

37. Sheep grazing beside the old Shottisham Creek mouth, which was an oyster fishery before it was dammed off. Canada Geese were introduced to the Deben in about 1972. Before 1914 shepherds used to take sheep over the river walls to graze on the saltings. This was done for the salt to improve fertility before the ewes went to the rams. The saltings were also used as a cure for foot and mouth disease.

37a. The Ramsholt 'Arms' in 1908. The shelters to the left of the 'Arms' were built to serve afternoon tea to visitors arriving by horse and carriage. The leisure industry had arrived on the Deben.

WORKING RIVER DEBEN

1. Melton Mill. Limit of the tidal waters.

2. Wilford Wharf was used to import road making material for the East Suffolk County Council until about 1935.

3. Melton Dock. Built about 1840. Dock for maltings. Last barge here about 1931. Houseboats and boatyard started here in the late 1950s. In 1987 Mel Skeet started floating pontoons which progressed on to the Granary Yacht Harbour. In 1968 Dick Larkman purchased marshes just above the Dock and began a yard which stores and maintains sailing yachts.

4. Melton Hill Dock. Dock for Melton Hill Maltings. Barge traffic finished about 1922. Yacht centre in 1964; later houseboats.

5. Sutton Hoo mounds.

6. Sun Wharf. A Dutch owned company imported coal here until the Woodbridge Canning Company bought the wharf and coal business. Last freight to Woodbridge was coal to this dock in 1940.

7. Lime Kiln Quay. The lime kilns were here in 1697 until late nineteenth century.

8. Gladwell's Dock. This is where local memory places the 'old wooden slip' down which Taylor launched trading schooners until 1853. Known as Harte's Dock, where coal came in and big oak trees were shipped out before 1914.

9. Mrs Robertson's swimming pool, 1924–40. This had a mud bottom and the water was changed daily from the river.

10. Lime Kiln Yard. Men-of-war were built here between 1624 and 1700. Merchant brigs and schooners, up until 1853. After 1884 three generations of Robertson's built yachts here.

11. The Pan. Once barge blocks here and timber stored afloat on the mud.

12. Tide Mill Yacht Harbour. Formerly the mill pond, the yacht harbour dug for Claude Whissock in 1962–64 on the lines of those he had seen in Holland. Wyllie pond was created in 1982 for the restored Tide Mill.

13. Woodbridge Tide Mill.

14. Claude Whissock started a boatyard here in 1926. Whisstock Boatyard closed in 1984; reopened as Whisstocks and closed in 1991.

15. Low water ferry hard. The original ferry hards were just above the Tide Mill. These new hards were built in 1879. The Suffolk Coastal District Council renewed the post at the end of the town hard in about 1974, but later all local government bodies were reluctant to accept ownership. In 1984 the Sutton Hoo Society and Woodbridge Cruising Club repaired the hard, but it silted up again.

16. Frank Knights and Phillip Gouch started a boatyard in the former Eastern Counties Farmers' warehouses on Ferry Quay in 1948.

17. Town Dock. The 663 tons 4th rater *Kingfisher* was launched here in 1675. In about 1700 this dock was walled off. Smith ran a boatyard here until 1859 when the railway went through and the yard and salt pans were demolished.

18. Jessup's Quay warehouses, pulled down about 1870.

19. Woodbridge Cruising Club house, built 1988.

20. Everson's and Town's jetty. Everson's jetty was used in the 1850s to discharge coal from schooners. Before 1914 Skinner's barges discharged coal at this jetty. The smaller Town Jetty built about 1895 was presented to the town by Dr Hubert Airy.

21. Granary 1820 on stilts in the river. Later there was a coal yard here on the landward side of the river wall. In 1889 Alfred Everson started a boatyard here in sheds on top of the river wall. These were burnt down in 1912 and reopened as the Phoenix Works taking in the old coal yards. Eversons was run and owned by Peter Darby from 1969 until sold to Frank Knights (Shipwrights) Ltd in 1991, when it became their South Yard.

22. Deben Yacht Club house, built in 1935.

23. Hillen's Hard. Barges loaded coprolite, straw and hay here before 1900.

24. Kyson Hole. Deep part of the river where ships laid and discharged part of their cargoes into a lighter so that they could get up river to the Woodbridge quays.

25. Kingston Quay. Passengers to London by steamer in 1842. Also a brick kiln here, and ballast dug for ships.

26. Old wharf at the head of Martlesham Creek where ships loaded goods brought by horse and cart from Grundisburgh. The local tradition is that the bricks used to build the White House, Washington, were

shipped from here and Kyson to the London River and then on to the USA.

27. Martlesham Creek. A few yachts here in the 1930s. In 1960 Ray Ingham bought the woods and started to develop the boatyard.

28. Loder's Cut. Dug in 1879 to avoid the difficulties ships had getting up Troublesome Reach.

29. The Horse. Woodbridge schooner's 'voyages' officially started and finished here. Once above this no food was given to the crews and if forced to anchor they landed on Kyson Point and walked home.

30. Bantam Dock. Farm trade until 1914.

31. Methersgate Dock. Small warehouse and farm trade until 1918.

32. Stonner Quay. Channel deepened and the quay built about 1850 by Thomas Waller to ship out coprolite and farm products. In the 1930s there was a low water channel behind Stonner Island for small boats.

33. Waldringfield cement works 1870–1908. Mason's barges brought coke and chalk from the Thames to the jetty and returned with cement. In 1921 Harry Nunn started boat building on the quay and later Nunn Bros built yachts here. In 1984 Reg Brown's passenger boat *Jahan* started running river trips from the new jetty.

34. Waldringfield Beach. Coprolite shipped out until all the Deben side pits closed in 1893. Barges brought muck from London street horses and returned with straw and hay until 1914. Imported Norwegian timber sold off the beach in 1916. In the 1930s Quantrill, Turner and Newson ran pleasure boats off the beach.

35. Girlings Hard on the Sutton shore. A ferry ran from here to the hard opposite, over Hemley Point saltings. This was used to collect Sutton and Ramsholt men who worked at the Waldringfield cement works. Waldringfield Sailing Club's racing buoy in the Bowship's Reach corrupted Girlings to the more romantic Galleons. In 1940 the Lowestoft smack *Colinda* was sunk by ice on the Waldringfield side.

36. Shottisham Creek. In 1760 the Ramsholt Estate started an oyster fishery in the old Shottisham Creek. After a big tide in 1904 broke through most of the Deben river walls this creek mouth was walled off.

37. Hemley Point. Mud dug for cement works.

38. Rocks Reach. Cattle were swum across to go to Ipswich Market.

39. Hemley Dock dug for farmer Cooper about 1897 for two barges to load farm produce.

40. Kirton Creek. Dock built at the head about 1880 for the brickyard. Barges brought in muck for farms until about 1933.

41. Ramsholt Dock. Dock was built to ship coprolite, then straw and hay, out. Alderton coal merchant had a coal store until the 1920s in the area, which became the dinghy park in the 1960s. The last cargo was sugar beet out to Cantley in about 1926.

42. Green Point oyster storage pits dug about 1882 near oyster beds in the channel.

43. Falkenham Creek wharf built about 1870 for barges which loaded straw and hay for London street horses. Not used after 1914.

44. Blackstakes. First water skiers' jetty in about 1977.

45. The Victorian thatched boathouse and Water Bailiff's cottage was slightly higher up King's Fleet than the present anglers headquarters. Like the Commissioner's Cottage down at the sluice the last of the boat house was ruined by the 1953 Floods.

46. Horse Sand. The Old Norse name horse means a bank in the middle of a channel. A little sand was loaded from here until 1946.

47. Alderton brick kiln had coal brought up the Bawdsey Fleet by barge until about 1860.

48. Bawdsey Quay. Built about 1890 for materials to be brought in to build Bawdsey Manor. Until 1914 coal came in for the Manor and its greenhouses. In about 1957 jetties were built for the ferry.

49. The Bawdsey lifeboat was kept in a boathouse on the point between 1825 and 1852. After this had been withdrawn the Passifuls owned a salvage yawl which was kept across the Haven on the Felixstowe shore.

50. Shingle was loaded off the beaches for ballast by outward bound Woodbridge schooners. Robert Skinner's barges loaded shingle on the Knolls for sale in Woodbridge up to his death in 1935. Ted Marsh continued the shingle trade until 1939.

51. The Monument pre-1914–89. A post put up as a tide gauge for the Harwich pilots. Ferry fishermen enjoyed telling summer visitors it was Nelson's Monument.

52. Walton Castle.

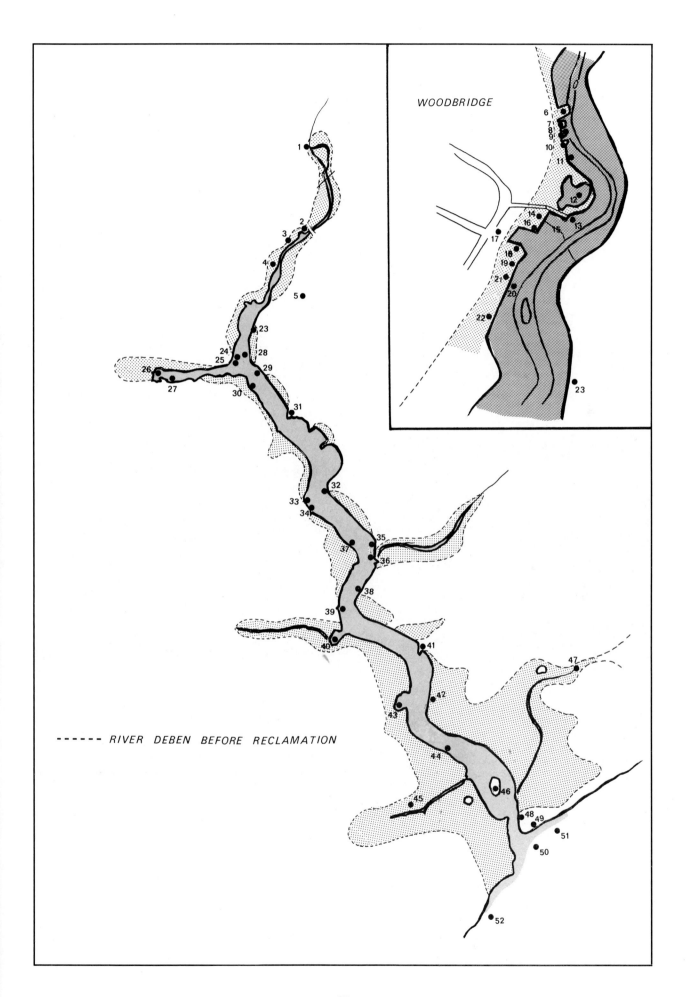

WOODBRIDGE

------ RIVER DEBEN BEFORE RECLAMATION

29

Chapter Four
FISHERMEN AND FERRIES

38. One of Charlie Stoker's smacks off Waldringfield. Every summer between about 1890 and 1924 smacks from West Mersea used to come into the Deben after oysters in the Ramsholt Reach, and eels, mostly above the Tide Mill. In the late summer the eels were likely to make a 'run' up into the freshwater river. At weekends the smacks were left anchored off the Ferry Dock and the crews went home by train. The Woodbridge boats had wet wells for storing eels which were found in the long eel grass seaweed. The eel grass suddenly died off in the 1920s and rain water running off the newly tarmaced roads was blamed. In the winters during the 1930s four Waldringfield men gathered cockles and mussels and graded them on the beach. This was revived in 1978 by Ray Lord, the Waldringfield harbour master. His successor, Alan Davidson, continued until 1986 but by that time TBT yacht antifoul had killed off the cockle beds so he switched to establishing oysters. Another small river shellfishery had grown up at about 1910–20 when 'Kaio' Collins of Alderton used to gather winkles on the Ramsholt flats and sell them round the villages on a donkey. Most of these shellfish seem to have vanished.

The medieval fishing in the river was achieved with flood and ebb 'kettles', wicker fish traps set up on the mud flats. In 1603 the Ramsholt Reach is described as 'hooking ground for whitings' where the Woodbridge fishermen 'resort in their season'. Very few fish actually breed in the river so the Deben is dependent on North Sea stocks. Overfishing at sea has reduced fish stocks, so the fishing in the river has also declined.

39. Isaac Ford and his wife Sarah near his boat *Pegasus* in 1903 at East Lane, Bawdsey. Some of the Bawdsey fishermen sold their catch round the villages but they sent their East Lane whelks to Billingsgate Fish Market. To reach the London train at Felixstowe the fishermen used to cross the ferry with their catch in sacks on their bicycles. The Bawdsey men gave up working from the beach in 1939 and after this the Ford family worked a boat from the Ferry, in summer mostly taking trips from the Dip around the Cork lightship.

40. David Brown of Felixstowe Ferry catching mullet off Shottisham Creek in 1988. Mullet were originally speared, but in the 1960s boats from outside the river came with drift nets and made large hauls. After this local boats fitted out for summer mullet fishing.

41. One of the fresh fish stalls at Felixstowe Ferry in 1971. The Felixstowe Ferry fishermen mainly fish at sea and the number of men involved varies between five and fifteen depending on profitability of the catches being landed. Fitting power hauling gear meant that by the mid-1980s most boats could be worked single handed.

The sixty-seven Felixstowe Ferry residents have fought very hard to stop development here. To further this aim Rob Ward organized the Felixstowe Ferry Foreshore Trust in 1992 which bought this foreshore from the Lord of the Manor. The Deben valley has mostly escaped development because the land owners have been devoted to farming and pheasant shooting.

42. The Bawdsey chain ferry. In this century the river has been a barrier between the villages on either side, but in the past when people walked there were more ferries, and also more contact. At Bawdsey, horses used to swim across and passengers crossed in a rowing boat until Sir Cuthbert Quilter opened up the steam chain ferries. Between 1894 and 1931 the Quilter Estate operated a chain ferry service, known as the 'Bridges', for vehicles between the Bawdsey and Felixstowe shores. The landing places for this ferry service are still clearly visible. It was a rule that if any member of the Quilter family appeared on either side wanting the ferry it had to go back and get them at once, even if the ferry was nearly across.

43. Robert Brinkley operating the Bawdsey ferry with the *Late Times*. After the chain ferry closed Charlie Brinkley, Robert's grandfather, ran a ferry service with a launch and later with his son Charlie until 1939. The ferry was closed for the war and Maurice Read got the RAF contract after the war. In 1962 Charlie Brinkley junior got the contract back and operated the ferry with *Delia* and then had the 28ft *Odd Times* built in 1963, the *Our Times* in 1963 and *Late Times* in 1969; the last two were built at the Felixstowe Ferry Boatyard. When RAF Bawdsey closed in 1974 the full time service ended, but the Brinkleys continued the ferry at summer weekends. John White, son-in-law, ran the ferry for two summers and Robert returned as ferryman in 1981. Most of the week he fishes with the *Odd Times* while the *Our Times* is kept as a spare.

44. Mrs Johnnie Perry, wife of the Mayor of Woodbridge, naming the new Woodbridge ferry boat *Saxon* with a horn of ale in 1985. The Ferry was reopened by the Sutton Hoo Society for people to visit the excavations. This service ran for five years and on its best day carried over hundred people, but it was never economically viable.

Woodbridge Ferry was a very ancient crossing for people coming on foot from the Sandlings villages. Between 1920 and 1947 Dick Elvin, born 1882, paid for the right to operate the ferry. The ferry service ran on demand between 7am and 9pm every day of the year except Christmas Day. Frank Knights took over the ferry and on one hot summer's day put across over 300 people, but buses killed the service. The Woodbridge Urban Council ran the ferry at a loss and wanted to close it, but the ferry right had been given to them in 1919 on the understanding that the ferry continued. Because the people living in the cottages near Ferry Farm used the ferry to go shopping, a local landowner, Mr Pelly, took their case all the way to the House of Lords in 1951 and forced Woodbridge Town to maintain the ferry. They employed George Skinner, last of the barging family, as ferryman. Officially the ferry ran until 1974, but it was actually allowed to fade out before.

Chapter Five
ALONG THE DEBEN TIDE LINE

45. A train crossing the iron bridge at Melton where the Deben is still tidal.

Opposite: 46. Cliff Hoppitt's aerial view taken in 1983, looking down river over Wilford Bridge towards Flea Island and down to Melton Dock. Flea Island is just saltings although in the early 1990s a man did live on it. The Sutton marshes on the left returned to tidal water during World War II when a bomb broke the river wall at Hackney Hole, on the bend below Melton Dock. This tidal lagoon has become a favourite place for cormorants to roost in the winter. As many as seventy, some ringed in Holland, have been counted here. Similar flooded marshes down the Deben are feeding grounds for grey herons or 'harnsers', to give them their Suffolk name.

The gravel and sand along the upper tidal Deben has been dug for the building trade since the 1930s. This started in Wilford Hill above Wilford Square (the roundabout) and probably removed the site of the public gallows where criminals of the Wilford Hundred were once hanged. In the 1970s at Bromeswell, George Green, the cricket bat willow merchant, had a pit dug beside the Deben which supplied material for the USAF Bentwaters runway. This pit has been turned into an attractive angling centre. Digging started on the marshes of Decoy Farm, on the bottom right, in the late 1980s and these have also been turned into an angling centre.

47. A view of Woodbridge in about 1912 across Gladwell's Dock past a warehouse to Robertson's Lime Kiln Yard. Berthed off Robertson's is one of the early houseboats. Frank Gladwell took over the coal business in 1923, but always had his coal delivered by rail. He let the dock to Robertson's for ten shillings a week and they charged people two shillings and sixpence a week to keep yachts there. However the Gladwells did not like people walking in the garden of their bungalow so they stopped the arrangement. Mrs Robertson was furious and did not speak to the Gladwells for years.

48. The *2605*, an Air Sea Rescue Launch built in 1943. During World War II she was used to rescue pilots shot down in the Mediterranean. The *2605* came to the Deben in 1972, and here in 1991 she was the home of artist Lil Tudor Craig, who led the campaign to keep the fifteen houseboats in the Melton reaches above Sun Wharf. In the background are the remains of the 85ft sailing barge *Westall* which came to the Deben as a houseboat in 1985. After being abandoned by her owners she was set on fire to clear the area, but the fire brigade arrived and would not allow it to burn.

49. A winter scene in Woodbridge in 1959 with Robert Simper's *Sea Fever* and Philip Allen's *Corista*. The *Sea Fever* was a 28ft ship's lifeboat converted to a gaff cutter by Ron Bayly at Felixstowe Ferry in 1953.

50. Woodbridge in 1957 with the old mill pond.

51. Drag lines starting work on constructing the Tide Mill Yacht Harbour in 1962.

52. In 1964 the Tide Mill Yacht Harbour was just being finished. The saltings just up river were filled in with the spoil when this marina was dredged in 1990.

53. Tide Mill Yacht Harbour in 1981.

54. A newspaper cutting of the 'Boat Inn' which closed in 1957. The 'Ship Inn' (now Small Craft Deliveries) closed in 1910. Only the 'Anchor' remains of the trilogy of Woodbridge sailors' pubs. In Victorian times farewell parties were held on the Anchor Green across the road when a Woodbridge ship was about to sail on a long voyage.

55. Fred Flegg and A. P. Waller in a boat on Waldringfield beach in 1885 with the cement works in the background. The Waller family were ship owners at Bawdsey and Goseford in the medieval period. By the eighteenth and early nineteenth centuries there were Wallers owning and farming land in Ramsholt and Sutton, but the family moved to Waldringfield where they then owned land. After 1862 four generations of the Waller family have been rectors of Waldringfield church.

56. Kyson Point in 1984 before the great public outcry in 1990 when the Point was fenced off. Trees on Kyson Point hide the pit dug for ballast for the schooners. Kyson Point was linked to the Market Hill by an ancient path across Broom Hill and Warren Hill called the Pilot's Way. The 1870s pilot Mark Taylor used to watch from Warren Hill to see the square-rigged timber ships coming in over the Bar and then row down to meet them. Later pilots could see a barge's topsail coming in over the Bar, but when the woods were planted at Ramsholt they could only see to the Rocks Reach. From then on they just used a shelter down on the river wall.

57. The Rev. John Waller's motor cruiser *Jesus* with Waldringfield 'Maybush' in the background. John Waller was mate on a sailing barge and then in deep-water ships before entering the church. He is keen on trawling in the cruiser.

41

58. On the left of the 'twizzler' in the Waldringfield 'Maybush' is George Turner and on the right is Jimmy Quantrill. In the l930s these two watermen let out moorings and ran pleasure boats from the beach. The 'Maybush' has been enlarged, but the twizzler is still in its original place. This was spun to see who bought the drinks and at Christmas they gambled for a pig with the numbers on the twizzler.

Jimmy Quantrill was one of Paul's barge skippers trading into the river. He took a liking to Waldringfield and became the landlord of the 'Maybush'. Every weekday morning at 5.30 beer was brought up from the cellar in a bath and 50 pints stood ready on the bar for the cement workers who walked in from Nacton, Brightwell, Ramsholt and other villages. The workers settled up their debt at the end of the week. George Turner had been cook on the royal yacht *Britannia* at the same time as his father Thomas Turner was skipper of this cutter. The 'Maybush' Inn was called the 'Cliff' Inn in 1827 and then the 'Bush' and at the beginning of this century had a blacksmith's shop on the car park end.

59. Waldringfield beach in about 1938.

60. Waldringfield at Whitsun in 1930. There are very few moorings and Jimmy Quantrill is just rowing alongside his motor boat.

61. Hemley in 1983 looking over towards Hemley Point. This is the largest area of saltings in Suffolk and a home to over a thousand wading birds. A third of all the saltings in the county are on the Deben.

62. Kirton Creek in 1984. The lonely barge hulk is the *Three Sisters*, which came up here and discharged muck for the Sluice Farm about 1932. She was in such poor order that the crew refused to take her to sea again and walked home to Ipswich.

63. The barge *Wolsey* on a yachting trip, with Ramsholt church in the background; about 1954. This church is on the site of the Anglo-Saxon village. Local tradition said that seamen once rowed up the creek below the church, now the Dock Marshes, to collect water from a well near the 'Anchor' Inn in the Vale of Ramsholt. The pub was moved, probably about 1820, to the 'Dock Inn' beside the road down to the quay.

64. Miss K. E. Waller at Ramsholt Dock in 1888 with her bull terrier Tip.

65. The 37ft smack yacht *Dawn*, built by Robertson in 1921, passing the Ramsholt 'Arms' shortly after Claude Whisstock bought her in 1947. On the opposite shore the Ramsholt ferry hard can still be seen. The small end of the 'Arms' was built as a ferryman's house in the eighteenth century and the ferry ran until about 1905. The house became Dock Farm and there was a coal business and chicory maltings here. In about 1906 the licence of the 'Dock Inn', which was just up the road, was moved down here and the squire turned this into a hotel with the more stylish name of 'Ramsholt Arms'. Because it started off as a hotel the 'Arms' has never had a public house sign. Until 1939 some visitors returned regularly to stay every summer. For about forty years the 'Arms' was kept by Dennis Nunn and then his widow, the redoubtable Mrs Nunn. In 1957 Sir Raymond Quilter had the extension built at the front and started to develop the 'Arms' for visitors who arrived by car.

66. Arthur Boyd sketching Shottisham Creek in 1991. This internationally known Australian artist has had the thatched cottage beside the Deben at Ramsholt since 1970.

67. Yachts fitting out at Ramsholt Dock in 1957. In the centre is Eric Burley's Dutch hoogaars *Tenace*. Behind her is Eric Burlingham's *Nimrod*, then across the dock *Sea Fever*, and also on the other side is the Rev. Will Groom's barge yacht *Marietta*. The *Marietta* sank off Ramsholt in 1967 on the same day as her owner's death.

68. George Collins, the Ramsholt harbour master, comes from a family who have lived in the Sandlings for many generations. His father George Collins (1904–83) was laying moorings at Ramsholt in the 1950s when there were about 25 boats here. When the mooring committee started in 1961 George senior became harbour master. In twenty years the number of moorings rose to 200, and it was decided not to increase them. All the three lower river mooring committees were under considerable pressure to fill the river with moorings, but are reluctant to turn the river into a massive boat parking area.

69. The 'Ferry Boat' Inn at Felixstowe Ferry in about 1903. The old Bawdsey rowing ferry ran from a creek which is now filled in but was behind these houses and was reached by the track behind the 'Ferry Boat'.

70. The 'meets' or pilot's marks at Felixstowe Ferry in 1908. The channel over the shingle bar across the entrance of the River Deben moves constantly. Boats crossing the Bar keep in the channel by lining up the 'meets', two posts. The 'meets' have to be shifted every year as the channel moves.

71. The Deben entrance with the bar channel on the right in about 1963. The bar channel is moved by prolonged SE gales, usually in the winter. Over a 9–14 year cycle the channel moved from north to south. This seems to have slowed down after the late 1960s, possibly because the seashore defences stopped the movement of shingle.

72. Bottom right is Bawdsey Manor in 1985. For centuries the farms and villages along either side of the Deben were the property of many different land owners, but in the Victorian period two men dominated the area. Colonel George Tomline's Orwell Park Estate owned much of the land on the Felixstowe peninsula, which reached the Deben at Felixstowe Ferry and Martlesham Creek, while on the eastern Sandlings shore Sir W. Cuthbert Quilter, a successful London stockbroker, bought, mostly from Lord Rendlesham, all the land from Bawdsey to Methersgate Hall to create the Bawdsey Estate.

In the 1880s Sir Cuthbert Quilter pulled down a Martello Tower and Battery on the Bawdsey point and built his country residence, Bawdsey Manor, overlooking the river mouth. The public road had run on the high ground right past the Manor to the ferry, but Quilter had a new road built out on the marshes. In 1937 the Quilters sold Bawdsey Manor and moved to Sutton. The Manor was bought by the Government for Sir Watson Watt to develop 'radio location' into radar. By World War II Bawdsey was an RAF radar station, part of the 'home chain' system which helped their pilots win the Battle of Britain. After the war it was a radar training station and the 325ft high Bawdsey pylons were pulled down in 1969. The station closed in 1974. It was reopened in 1979 as RAF Bawdsey surface-to-air missile unit, which closed in 1991.

73. Martello Tower T, built about 1810, and the last RAF Bawdsey pylon are reminders that the Suffolk coast has for centuries been in the front line of any threatened invasion from Europe.

50

74. The Cherub *Sea Pig* in Woodbridge Haven in 1989. Where the shingle is in the foreground there was a channel which was used by fishing boats ten years before.

75. The Cork lightship with Harwich pilots alongside for a cup of tea in 1973. Two years later the Cork Light was replaced by a LANBY (Large Automatic Navigation Buoy).

Chapter Six

THE BOAT BUILDERS

THE EARLIEST ship in the Deben area is the 89ft longship found in the Sutton Hoo mounds. It is more than likely that this Anglo-Saxon ship was actually built on the Deben. The most likely place where a ship of this size could have been launched into deep water was either Kyson Point or the site of the present Lime Kiln yard at Woodbridge. Silting has altered the upper reaches and by the eighteenth century the only deep water for launching at Woodbridge was the Lime Kiln yard. Commercial ships were built here until 1853. There was then a break until Ebenezer Robertson bought the yard in 1884 and restarted building on the Deben. After this, boat building slowly snowballed. Men who had trained at Robertson's, such as Everson, Whisstock and Knights, all started their own yards. The process kept going and Claude Whisstock used to remark that most of the next generation of Deben shipwrights had been trained in his yard.

By the 1960s there were nine places along the Deben where wooden hulls could be built, and at four of these they still can. The other great standby of the Deben was building new wooden clinker beach boats for the Suffolk fisherman and these are still built. Trevor Moore at the Felixstowe Ferry Boatyard built many and in 1989 Frank Knights (Shipwrights) started building beach boats again.

76. 'Robbie' Robertson with one of the early launches he built at Lime Kiln yard, Woodbridge, in about 1910.

52

77. Barge yacht under construction at the Lime Kiln yard 1910. Robertson became well known for building barge yachts designed by E. B. Tredwen.

78. A barge yacht being built at Robertson's about 1911.

79. The barge yacht *Esnia* at the Lime Kiln yard in 1911.

80. One of the early power boats on the Deben just after launching at Robertson's, about 1910.

81. John Russell White recaulking *L'Atalanta* in 1978 in the almost empty Lime Kiln yard. John White was then a freelance shipwright. The Kestrel Shed, where the wooden Kestrel class were built at Robertson's, was being used by Mike Clark for his boat building business in the 1990s.

82. The *Corista* sailing off Bawdsey, with the radar pylons of RAF Bawdsey in the background. The *Corista* was built by Whisstock in 1952 to a design by 'Jack' Francis Jones of Waldringfield.

83. Bill McFadden, Claude and Joan Whisstock getting the ribbon ready on the bottle before the launching of the 46ft 26 ton *Corista* in 1952. Building a wooden yacht of this size and quality meant that Whisstock had become one of the leading yacht builders in Britain.

This yard was started by Claude Whisstock (1903–90) in 1926 on what was then a piece of marsh behind Ferry Quay. The first workshop was on stilts, and although the marsh was filled in and had river frontage, it was not near deep water and the yard often had trouble in launching boats off the slipway.

The first sizable craft Whisstock built was in 1929 and after this the yard continued to build new wooden yachts. This included their own Deben four tonner class of which the first was launched in 1931 and the last in 1953. The 15 ton ketch *Landfall*, yard no 409, which Claude built for himself in 1958, was the beginning of another new class. The next two decades the yard was busy: as well as with storage and repair, with building 'one off' yachts. The largest was the 25 ton motor ketch *Sun Cloud* in 1969. By that time most yards had given up trying to build wooden hulls, but Claude was determined to continue and cornered a very limited market, even though this policy of 'new build' rather than repair work became increasingly difficult commercially. Whisstock's continued wooden boat production with the Naja class, using a new wood epoxy saturation technique, and about 30 Najas were produced.

The last wooden hull yacht built was the 45ft wood epoxy schooner *Calisto* in 1983. After 1979 the yard increasingly specialized in aluminium alloy yachts. To start with the hulls were built elsewhere and just fitted out at the yard. In 1984 the first aluminium hull, the 62ft *Blest*, was built at the yard for B. A. Lester.

Unfortunately the yard was forced to close in April 1984, but George Whisstock, Claude's son, was instrumental in reopening the yard as Whisstock's Ltd in May 1985. The new company continued the new build policy, but turned to larger one-off aluminium yachts such as the the 55ft schooner *Red Jack* in 1987 and the 85ft luxury motor yacht *Gitala*, yard no 518, in 1988. At the height of the recession in 1991 the lack of orders finally closed this yard and all the thirty two people working there lost their jobs.

84. Launching of Claude Whisstock's 16 ton ketch *Landfall* in 1958.

85. In 1966 The Whisstock Boatyard celebrated forty years of boat building at Woodbridge. Front row, L to R, Mary East, George, Joan, Claude and Susan Whisstock, Russell Upson and Jane Whisstock. Second row, L to R, John Nichols, Dennis Hayles, 'Archie' Rose, Dick Youngman, 'Wally' Howe, 'Tim' Tight, John Krejsa, Ken Garnham, Bill McFadden, 'Benny' Battle and John Nunn. Back row, L to R, Ray Evans, Alan Dale, 'Bob' Gearing, Michael Simmons, Peter Benstead, John Broadbent and Graham Challis.

86. George and Claude Whisstock at their yacht harbour in 1971.

87. The wooden ketch *Matapan* being launched from Whisstock's in 1971 with the gasometer and St John's Church tower in the background.

88. Alan Dale, the Whisstock rigger, with the work boat, towing the newly launched *Matapan* away.

89. Launching the *Rum' u' Ginger* from Whisstocks in 1990. After her was the *Windward Dream*, the last to be launched at Whisstock's, although two uncompleted hulls were taken away to be fitted out.

90. The Cornish pilot *Bluejay* being launched at Robertson's in 1988. About 1985 Mike Illingworth and Adrian Overbury took over running Robertson's and revived the yard.

91. Philip Gouch in the smack *Quiz*, which was originally built in 1872 and then rebuilt by Frank Knights Shipwrights in 1979.

92. The relaunch of the smack *Yet* in 1989 with Frank Knights and Keith Cutmore. Frank Knights bought the *Yet* out of fishing at Brightlingsea in 1938. After returning from being in the Royal Navy during World War II Frank and Christine lived aboard the smack in the Ferry Dock for several years. To celebrate owning the *Yet* for fifty years they brought her ashore at Ferry Quay and gave her a major refit.

93. A. A. Everson started his boat building business at Woodbridge in 1889 and it was continued by his sons Cyril and Bert as Everson and Sons Ltd until 1969. Two of A. A. Everson's daughters did the yard's office work. They lived in a shed behind the river wall until this was demolished by the 1953 floods. They then moved into the Chandlery on the river wall and lived in amongst the yacht stores until the yard was sold.

94. John Alexander's new Tomahawk 25 being launched by Di Alexander at Everson's in 1972. This yard, like Robertson's, had switched to fitting out fibreglass hulls. A decade before, Everson's were building wooden yachts: the *Glee* in 1960, Michael Spear's C. R. Holman-designed *Maleni* in 1962 and then the *Golden Samphire* in 1963.

95. Dick Larkman driving his 15 ton crane at his Melton boatyard. Dick started at Whisstock's in 1947, then worked for Nunn's before starting to build boats at Waldringfield in 1960. Later he bought some marshes off Bill Boss at Melton and by using a crane, not a slipway, to launch boats was able to develop a yard. The yard employs Dick and Dawn Larkman and their sons Steven and 'Fred'. Dick declined to have his photo taken for this book and said 'we don't exist, we just get customers!' Actually this low profile yard had stored 173 sailing yachts in the winter 1991–92.

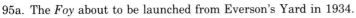

95a. The *Foy* about to be launched from Everson's Yard in 1934.

Chapter Seven

YACHTS AND THE BOAT PEOPLE

96. A group of yachts gathering for a Deben Yacht Club race at Woodbridge, about 1910. One of the yachts in this group appears to be the *Syren*, which was built at Woodbridge in 1842 and sailed on the river for over seventy years. The *Syren* carried a cannon that was used to start Deben Yacht Club races. She was owned by Mr A. Gall, who owned a chemist shop in the Thoroughfare, and was looked after by his one legged paid hand 'Peg' Gray. Part of the paid hand's job was to row the yacht home if the wind dropped.

97. The 'flag ship of the Deben', *Clytie*, being laid up by Everson's in about 1968. She is the longest-resident yacht on the Deben. Built by Everson's in 1922 for Sir Clifford Paterson, who was the first Commodore of the Waldringfield and Hemley Sailing Club when it started in 1921. This yacht had replaced his previous *Clytie*, which had been built by Robertson's in 1913.

98. The 21ft Cherub class racing at Bawdsey about 1938. On the right are *Wild Rose* and *Jubilee*. The Cherub seems to have been the first cabin class built on the east coast. The class started with the slightly smaller *Dream* in 1923, which was modelled on the Bombay Tomtit and was intended to be hauled up Aldeburgh beach. Between 1924 and 1937 eighteen Cherubs were built by Everson's.

99. Christine and Frank Knights aboard their smack *Yet* in 1988.

100. Peter Darby's steam yacht *Myra*, built in 1893, has been based at Woodbridge since 1979.

101. Geoffrey Ingram-Smith's Broads pleasure steamer *Yarmouth* laid up at Wilford Wharf in 1972 before becoming a museum ship at the Tide Mill. The hut near Wilford Bridge was manned by staff of Hollesley Bay Borstal every time boys escaped.

102. Hys Orlik 's Dutch steel paviljoentjalk *Neljan*, built about 1900. Since 1981 she has been based in the Tide Mill Dock as a charter vessel.

103. Another flat bottomed Dutch craft that made her home on the Deben is the *Windhaver*. She was built in about 1903 and bought from the fishing fleet on the eastern shore of the Ijsselmeer in about 1965.

104. George Arnott, the Woodbridge auctioneer, aboard *L'Atalanta* which he kept on the Deben from 1937–67. He started the Woodbridge Spring Boat Sales, was a local historian and an active spokesman for any campaign to stop the area from changing.

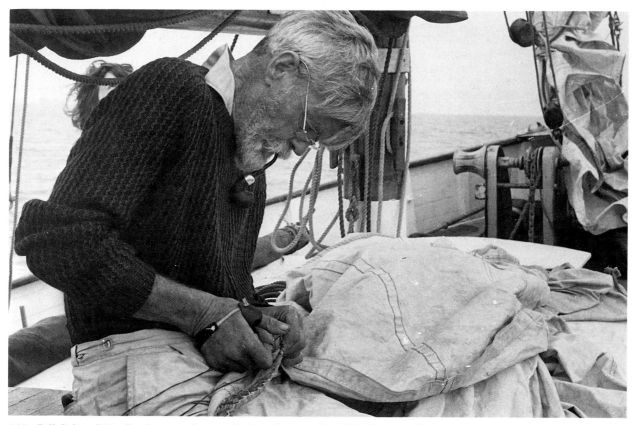

105. Bill Coke of Woodbridge mending a sail aboard the ex Swedish Customs Cutter *L'Atalanta* in 1975. Bill's parents had lived aboard the elegant Edwardian racing yacht *Mariquita* in the Ferry Dock. Bill sailed all over the world but always returned to the Deben.

106. The *Try Again*, owned by Graham Pool and sailed by his son David, anchored in the Rocks Reach. She was built as a 3 masted lugger on Guernsey in about 1870 and rebuilt in 1900 and again in 1957. The following year she came to the Deben and has spent every winter in the Ferry Dock and the summer on a mooring at Kyson Point.

107. The Rev. F. Leeder's 14ft Kingfisher *Shelduck* in about 1978. During World War II a Norfolk Broads dinghy was stored in Everson's shed. Everson's took the lines off this and created the DYC's Kingfisher class. Between 1943 and 1963 twenty-nine Kingfishers were built and they raced as a class until 1966.

108. David Scott Cowper provisioning his 29ft Wanderer *Airedale*, in the Tide Mill Yacht Harbour, for the 1976 Trans-Atlantic Single Handed Race. This was the beginning of a series of incredible single handed ocean voyages, which have all begun at Woodbridge. David Cowper set up eighteen records, more than any other yachtsman.

David Cowper, from Melton, brought his 41ft aluminium hull Huisman *Ocean Bound* to Whisstock's to be fitted out and then in 1979–80 made a 225 day single handed circumnavigation, beating Sir Francis Chichester's and Dame Naomi James' times and establishing a new record. In 1982 David made a second circumnavigation but this time a far more hazardous route westward against the roaring forties and rounding all five southern capes. This took 219 days and established a new record.

While working on *Ocean Bound* at Whisstock's David noticed the 41ft ex-RNLI lifeboat *Mable E. Holland* and his attention turned from sail to power for a third voyage round the world. In 1984–85 he went in the *Mabel* via the Panama Canal and achieved the first ever single handed circumnavigation by a power craft, but still he dreamt of more record breaking voyages. So far David had been following in the wake of other great single handed sailors, but in his 1986–90 circumnavigation he was the first person to go single handed through the North West Passage. During the first part of this voyage through the Canadian High Arctic to the Bering Sea David and the *Mabel* endured some of the worst weather in the world with temperatures falling to −57. The *Mabel* was constantly under pressure from the pack ice. She survived three Arctic winters, although when David returned in 1987 the *Mabel* was partly sunk. Totally alone and two hundred and fifty miles from the nearest settlement David salvaged the boat and got the two Gardiner engines working again. When he finally reached the Pacific the *Mabel* ploughed on reliably and after meeting some incredibly high seas off the Cape of Good Hope completed Cowper's fourth voyage back to the Deben.

109. In 1980 David Cowper returns triumphantly in his *Ocean Bound* after a record breaking single handed voyage round the world.

110. David Cowper on the *Mabel E. Holland* in 1984 before setting out on his first voyage in her.

111. The 37ft *Mirelle*, which was built by Whisstock's in 1937 and was based at Waldringfield for over forty years. *Mirelle* was designed by W. M. 'Max' Blake, who after running a boatyard in Singapore for 25 years returned to Suffolk and designed yachts for Whisstock's.

112. Sean McMillan sailing his gaff cutter *Thistle* at Waldringfield. In 1986 Sean started building wooden yachts to his own design in a small barn next to his cottage at Woodbridge.

113. The 30ft *Sea Rhapsody* built by 'Ernie' Nunn at Waldringfield in 1955 for Dr Kenneth Palmer.

114. George Turner of Waldringfield sailing Dragonfly 2 in a veterans' event. George's success as a racing helmsman started just after World War II and he carried on winning races for forty years in Dragonfly, Dragon and Squib classes. George regularly helmed Dragonfly 14, 3 and 38 before he eventually bought 35. Dragonfly sail numbers were issued up to about 45. This class was built by Nunn's, which were believed to be lighter and faster, and by Robertson's.

115. The 'Daily Express' cartoonist Carl Giles kept his *Circe* on a mooring off the 'Maybush', Waldringfield. Here she is taking part in the 1976 Procession up river for the annual Yachtsmen's Service on Waldringfield Beach.

116. Captain Gilbey, owner, and Arthur Hunt, professional skipper, sailing the *Genesta* up to her mooring at Ramsholt in 1953. This was the last of the old style yachting where the paid skipper maintained the yacht. Captain and Mrs Gilbey lived at Waldringfield and were collected in a small motor boat by Arthur and taken down to their yacht at Ramsholt.

117. Yachtsmen gathered in the Ramsholt 'Arms' kitchen for a laying up supper in 1960. From L to R the group includes Claude and George Whisstock, Ben Cooper, Eric Burlingham, Robert Simper, Michael Beeton, Harry and John Ballham, Dickie Standard, George Collins senior (wearing a peaked cap), Walter Hales, George Green and Norman Simper.

118. Charlie Brinkley putting Carl Giles back aboard his yacht at Felixstowe Ferry.

119. The *Girl Carole* taking part in the 1972 Fishing Boat Race. This race was started by the Felixstowe Ferry SC in 1970 to raise money for the RNLI. The winner was Trevor Moore's *Pat M*, second Peter Benstead's *Silver Cloud* and third Stephen Read's *Eileen C*.

119a. Off the Bawdsey Ferry shore in 1885 the Harwich tug *Commodore* has just finished towing in a Norwegian timber brigantine over the Deben Bar. Bad weather forced ships to shelter in Harwich Harbour and sometimes after this a tug was hired to tow them all or part of the way to Woodbridge.

Chapter Eight

GALES, HIGH TIDES AND HARD WINTERS

120. During the early hours of February 1, 1953, a massive tide breached the East Coast sea defences. At Felixstowe Ferry the huge tide pushed the shingle right across the road and the sea covered the golf course and through the Tomline Wall to the Felixstowe Marshes. All the Deben river walls broke, but luckily there was no loss of life on the river.

121. The river wall on the Ramsholt Dock Marshes being repaired after the salt water broke through in 1949. There was serious flooding on the fresh water and tidal Deben after the hard winter of 1947 and again in 1949. This resulted in a long programme of lining the river walls with concrete slabs with German prisoners of war doing much of the labouring work. Also the channel above Wilford Bridge was straightened. The walls had to be rebuilt again after the 1953 Flood.

122. The German coaster *Harle Strand* ashore at East Lane, Bawdsey, in 1977. She ran ashore here after engine trouble, but was towed off.

123. The Ferry Dock at Woodbridge frozen over in 1895. The crane in the centre was for loading tree trunks. This Dock has considerably silted up since then.

124. The Ferry Dock frozen in 1940. The West Country trading schooner *Isobel* was a house boat. The warehouses were still used by Eastern Counties Farmers, but were bought by the Woodbridge Quay Company in 1957.

125. Ice at Kyson Point early in 1963. The Deben was frozen over enough at Waldringfield for people to walk across, the only time it is known to have happened. Yachts laid up on the saltings at Woodbridge were carried down river in ice floats as far as the Rocks Reach.

126. A crashed B17 Flying Fortress hauled ashore in front of the Ramsholt 'Arms' in 1945. In February 1945 a brief break in the bad weather led the USAF to get every available bomber into the air for a massive raid intended to destroy the Nürnberg railway marshalling yards. Shortly after this B-17 Flying Fortress took off from Debach airfield heavily laden with bombs and fuel; one engine caught fire and the pilot found it impossible to keep in the air and ditched in the River Deben. The Flying Fortress landed on the river in front of the 'Arms' and sank at once. Eight of the crew were lost but the pilot got out and Arthur Hunt, who was on the quay getting ready for a day's fishing, went out and rescued him.

127. The crashed B17 and all her bombs and fuel sank in 18ft of water at Ramsholt. She was raised and hauled ashore by two tanks. and then broken up.

128. A service on Ramsholt Dock quay in 1992 with flags being lowered as USAF Veterans went out and placed wreaths on the river in remembrance of eight of their fellow servicemen who had been drowned here in the 1945 B17 crash.

129. In the early hours of the morning of October 16, 1987, for the first time for 250 years, a SW hurricane swept over south east England. At about 8am, at the tail end of the hurricane, the 35ft *L'Atalanta* is riding at her moorings in the Rocks Reach with spindrift being wipped off the wave tops to form a mist. The only damage was the strain of the mooring strop flattening the bow rail.

130. The majority of the yachts on the Deben received some damage or dragged their moorings ashore. On the morning after the hurricane yachts were ashore at Ramsholt; between Green Point and Pretyman's Point 37 yachts dragged ashore. At Felixstowe Ferry about 40 boats dragged ashore and three sank.

131. The greatest damage to yachts in the 1987 hurricane was at Woodbridge. At high water the largest waves ever seen in the upper reaches were sending clouds of spray over the ferry landing. In the Ferry Dock the yachts moored close together suffered severe chafing and several were insurance write-offs, while others broke lose and drifted ashore.

132. Low water after the hurricane. Boats sunk near Woodbridge Tide Mill.

132a. The tranquil summer scene looking across to Hemley Point gives no hint of the problems of rising sea levels. Since the late 1960s the saltings have steadily crumbled away and some have been lost to development. In the past the saltings and ooze were regarded as 'waste', but research has shown that these areas are all vital for the survival of the estuary's wild life. The Deben is very important for wading birds and wildfowl and is internationally important as the winter habitat of redshanks.

Chapter Nine

LEISURE RIVER

THE MAIN boating centres on the Deben are at Melton, Woodbridge, Kyson Point, Waldringfield, Ramsholt and Felixstowe Ferry. All these have their own special character created by the outlook of the people who live or take their leisure time at these landings. Everybody looks at the river in a completely different way. The sailing, water-skiing, wildfowling and canoeing clubs make very different uses of the same river. Many Deben river users don't join any club and like the river simply for the sense of freedom it gives them. Although in the summer the river is often very crowded it has not lost its ability to enchant those who know it. With the changes in weather and tides it is a different river every time you go near it.

133. The Deben Yacht Club at Woodbridge during its 150 year celebration sail-past in 1988. The regatta was started at Woodbridge in 1838 to mark the coronation of Queen Victoria. This became an annual event and the committee of local yachtsmen who organized it eventually turned it into the Deben's first yacht club.

135. The 'topping up' ceremony of the Woodbridge Cruising Club's new club house in 1988. Back, L to R, John White (Bosun); Mike Meister (Builder/Rear Commodore); Neville Allen (Vice Commodore); David Poole (Architect); front, L to R, Paul Bloom (PRO) and Don Smith (Commodore).

The Woodbridge Cruising Club started in 1965 in the back room of the 'Anchor' and later had a club room on the Ferry Quay. By 1992 the club had 340 members many of whom had joined in their main summer cruise to Belgium and Holland. The club had close links with Woubrugge in Holland and Lowestoft on this side of the North Sea.

136. Waldringfield dinghies returning to their dinghy park after their Saturday afternoon race in 1992. The Waldringfield Sailing Club was started in 1921. About 1947 the club started their 14ft Dragonfly class. It has also been very much a family club and is restricted to 650 members.

137. The Squib class racing at Waldringfield in 1972. Shortly after this the class became popular here and the Squibs largely replaced the Dragonflies and Dragons.

138. The *Dusmarie* off Kirton Creek in 1984, the year she celebrated her hundredth year. This Ramsholt-based gaff yawl cruised extensively when she was used as a sail training vessel and took part in the Tall Ships Races.

139. Fireballs racing at Felixstowe Ferry in 1973. Felixstowe Ferry Sailing Club started as a very small club for the local community and even had its own class, the 14ft Felixstowe Ferry One Design.

140. A 505 Championship organized by the Felixstowe Ferry Sailing Club. Dinghy racing first began at Felixstowe Ferry in the 1920s with International 12ft dinghies. The club, although quite informal was known as the Felixstowe Dinghy Club with a wing over water burgee design. The club sweaters carrying the letters FDC were never popular due to the confusion with Felixstowe District Council! In 1931 a group of Orwell based yachtsmen helped to found the Felixstowe Ferry Yacht and Dinghy Club in conjunction with the old Dinghy Club but there was much rivalry between the old dinghy and new yachting factions. The Club was renamed the Felixstowe Ferry Sailing Club in 1934.

In 1966 the Firefly National Championship was held at Felixstowe Ferry. For the next decade the club went through a tremendous period of success when it became internationally known. Many young sailors from the Deben area joined the Club for sea racing over the Deben Bar which was fun and highly competitive, and in addition the club had a very lively social life.

The success of sailing at Felixstowe Ferry has for many years revolved around the family White. Barry White, a Ferry fishermen became landlord of the 'Ferry Boat' and after his death was continued on by his wife Trudi for many years. Youngest son Peter White became World 505 Champion in 1970 with crew John Davies, in Hong Kong. This was probably the pinnacle of family success. However, brother David together with Peter were at the front end of International 505 and National Firefly fleets for many years and the backbone of local dinghy sailing. Sister Pam White must not be left out as she also made her name as a helm on the National Firefly circuit. To top this out senior brother John White, local boatyard director, brought Squib racing to Felixstowe Ferry in 1987 and started yet another successful phase of club racing.

141. The 1988 Lark Championships at the Felixstowe Ferry Sailing Club. The club house is also the headquarters of the East Suffolk Water Skiing Club. Since the 1930s sailing for leisure has been the main activity on the River Deben.